LARS ROOD

ARE YOU

RED

CUP

CHRISTIAN?

HOW TO LIVE A **STAND-OUT FAITH** IN A **FIT-IN** WORLD

simply for **students**

YouthMinistry.com/TOGETHER

Are You a Red-Cup Christian?
How to Live a Stand-Out Faith in a Fit-In World

© 2014 Lars Rood

group.com
simplyyouthministry.com

Credits
Author: Lars Rood
Executive Developer: Jason Ostrander
Chief Creative Officer: Joani Schultz
Editor: Rob Cunningham
Cover Art and Production: Laura Wagner and Veronica Preston

ISBN 978-0-7644-9006-4

10 9 8 7 6 5 4 3 2 1   20 19 18 17 16 15 14

Printed in the United States of America.

ACKNOWLEDGMENTS

In other books I've written, I don't think I've ever formally acknowledged the youth workers who were involved in my life growing up. They had a profound impact on me, especially during middle school and my first couple of years of high school. They loved me, always encouraged me, and made youth group a place that I always wanted to be. I hope that I model that to the students that I work with today.

I'd also like to thank my current Family Life Ministry team at Bellevue Presbyterian Church (Belpres) for being such a great team that really cares about young people and the transitions they make. With God's blessing, we will help kids grow into young adults who have a stand-out faith.

Lastly, I'd like to thank my family. I write because I feel called to it, and you have all supported me in many projects and made it so much fun to be transparent and honest. Thanks for continuing to encourage me to grow into the man of God that I'm supposed to be. My hope is that I model what I write about—and you four, above anyone else, have the freedom to call me out when I don't.

TABLE OF CONTENTS

PART 3: SOLUTIONS

INTRODUCTION

A few years ago I stood on a corner in Austin, Texas, watching thousands of college students stand around with red cups in their hands. At first I just wondered what they were all drinking. As I stood there I started reflecting on the hundreds of high school students who had graduated from youth ministries I had overseen. I began wondering how many of those students had likely been in similar situations in college— standing around with a red cup in their hand, looking like everyone else.

But as I thought about what I was witnessing, I became less interested in the beverages inside those cups and more focused on what those cups represented. I kept thinking about how no one really knows what's in that cup—just like no one really knows what's going on inside of us. We can easily end up looking like everyone else on the outside and can fall into the trap of becoming a "red-cup Christian."

Since that day in Austin, I have reflected a lot on students and their faith journey. I find myself wondering why some students had a walk with God that continued into adulthood while others, right after they graduated, seemed to just turn their backs on everything related to their faith.

As a youth pastor it's hard to watch people walk away from their faith. I've watched students— teenagers that I had spent all kinds of time with—just chuck it all and walk away. We had talked about doubts, we sang worship songs, I shared my heart, and I talked about the Bible. I had served alongside these teenagers locally and overseas, and I felt like I had done everything to give them a robust faith that would stay strong.

I thought I had a pretty good handle on what needed to be done to make faith stick. But how poorly I predicted future pathways, so much of the time. The teenager that I didn't expect to continue to walk with Jesus did—while the student leaders in our group were often the quickest to fall away.

I've written this book to encourage you to think deeply about your faith and to take some steps during high school to strengthen that faith before you graduate. This will take some work on your part because you will have to be honest, transparent, and real about things that are hard. You'll ultimately have to share your deepest struggles and thoughts with others as you move toward "being known" by other people.

This isn't about *looking* the part of a Christian. I'm not concerned with how you dress, what you look like, or any exterior trappings of how the world (or the church) thinks a Christ-follower must appear. Instead, my hope—and my prayer—is that you will see movement in the faith you claim and the heart for following Jesus that you've declared is important, that it will go from a place of being hidden inside of you to a place where people see it clearly when they get to know you because your heart is transparent.

The ultimate goal of this book is to encourage you to live a "stand-out faith in a fit-in world." The world wants you to act and live in a particular way, especially when you leave high school, but with a healthy mix of tips, wisdom, actions, and ideas, your faith can transcend what the world is expecting you to do.

We will embark on our journey by first looking at some of the problems we have all experienced when it comes to our faith. The goal isn't to poke holes in your faith or to point out flaws, but just to recognize some of the struggles you come up against and how they can affect you.

The second part of this book focuses on needs. We will examine specific things that you need in order to have a strong faith journey that will keep growing and will provide depth in your transition from high school to college, a career, or the military.

Lastly, we will look at solutions—some specific ideas and things that can help you learn more about having a stand-out faith journey in this world. This section might feel like a bunch of lists and ideas to try, but I've offered lots of suggestions because not everything will connect with everyone. But I'm confident you will connect with at least one thing there (probably more), even if some topics might not exactly fit your needs right now.

Here we go!

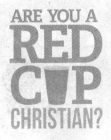

ARE YOU A
RED
CUP
CHRISTIAN?

PART 1
PROBLEMS

ARE YOU A

RED
C🥤P

CHRISTIAN?

Part of me hates writing this section because it'll seem like an indictment or sad testimony of our weak faith. But I am convinced we must begin with some stark reminders about some of the struggles we have with our faith. Many of us struggle to make Jesus a priority in our lives, and the habits you form *now* will continue with you beyond high school.

My goal isn't to beat you up. In fact, I hope that much of this first section doesn't describe you at all. I hope you already have things figured out and you are walking with Jesus in a deep and significant way. If that's the case, I still think you will benefit from reading this section because each chapter points out a pitfall that you could easily fall into during your faith journey. Use them as reminders of how to avoid getting caught up in trying to "fit in."

It's possible that you are like me and have gone through stages in your faith where some of these things in these chapters have been true. You've held things in and not allowed people to know your real feelings. You've focused too much on everything else you are doing and too little on your faith. View these topics as teaching times to help you avoid falling into the same traps again.

As you read through this section, I want to encourage you to allow the Holy Spirit to speak to you. Maybe it'll happen during a story or reflection time or even during the questions. If you allow all parts of this journey to sink in, I am confident that something will reach you.

CHAPTER 1:
ARE YOU LIKE A RED CUP?

A "SECRET" ABOUT RED CUPS

I recently taught a class to a bunch of youth workers at a national convention. To start out the class—and in an attempt to be funny—I showed a slide that explains the meaning for each line on a red Solo® cup. Each line, I told the group, reveals how much beer (12 ounces), wine (4 ounces), or liquor (2 ounces) to put in the cup. Some people who had never seen this slide before had no clue that these measurements existed. As I shared the info, they just nodded like it clearly made sense—because really, drinking alcohol is what those cups are for, right?

OK, time to come clean: The company doesn't actually put the lines on the cups for any reason. (I made sure my youth worker friends knew that, too.) Those lines have been around for a long time, and it's just a coincidence that they line up at exact ounce markers—at least, all the research I've done says that it's a coincidence. But in many ways, it doesn't matter if it's true or not. These red cups have become an image that most people associate with parties and alcohol.

In the early days of social media, people seemed to have little concern about the types of pictures that they were willing to post and share. Back then, as a youth pastor wanting to stay connected to students after they graduated from high school, I would often check out their pages and accounts. Many times their pictures were filled with red cups, and because I associate those cups with partying, I couldn't help but be sad at the choices students were making.

But here's a crazy thing about those cups: A student could simply have filled theirs with some sort of soft drink and stood around with everyone else. Yet they would still be judged as if they were drinking with everyone else because they had the same kind of cup.

WHAT'S HAPPENING ON THE INSIDE?

We are often just like these red cups. We resemble everyone else on the outside, but no one really knows what's going on inside. I lived my faith like this for a long time. In high school I was a good youth group kid who never missed any of our group's events or activities. But on the inside I really wasn't following Jesus as much as my youth pastor thought I was. I went to youth group because it was my social scene and the place I felt most comfortable. But I was struggling to figure out who I was and what I believed. I went to all the parties and sometimes made bad choices that I would regret later. On the outside I was living one way that I wanted people to see, but on the inside I was living totally differently.

I want you to know that I realize and appreciate how tough things can be for you—our culture tells us to live and act in certain ways, and you want to "fit in" with the world (or at least with specific groups of people). It can be really tough if you don't feel like you belong or aren't a part of something. I'm not trying to tell you that you need to go out and buy every flavor of Christian T-shirt that exists or carry your Bible wherever you go. The goal here is to help you define what you are living for and figure out ways of taking those desires from the inside to the outside.

THINK ABOUT

I wonder how many of us have done something that we really don't want anyone else to know about. I'm guessing we all have stuff hidden deep down inside that we hope never gets out—all of us have things that we hide. But our faith isn't something we need to hide. Many people respect following Jesus. We sometimes can get all caught up in the negative images that people have of Christians. But I've found that if you simply say, "I really like Jesus and I'm following him," most people don't respond negatively.

QUESTIONS

1. How much of the "real you" do people see?

2. What holds you back from sharing the "true you" with others? When are you most likely to do this, and why?

3. How do you know if Jesus is truly important to your life right now? What might other people observe?

4. How well do you think your faith will transition to life after high school? Why?

CHAPTER 2:
DO YOU WANT PEOPLE TO KNOW WHAT'S INSIDE?

FINDING A PLACE OF SAFETY

I'm an introvert. But people who interact with me without knowing me very well often think I'm exactly the opposite. Growing up I felt more comfortable alone than with others, so I spent most of my childhood, middle school, and high school years locked away in my room reading. It was my "safe place" where no one could hurt me.

My family had moved right in the middle of my fourth-grade year, and it was a traumatic experience for me. I left behind an elementary school where I was well-liked and teachers who knew me, and moved to a place where I was an outsider from day one. It didn't help that I had a slightly odd name—people quickly figured out many ways of making fun of both "Lars" and "Rood." There weren't a lot of other kids who lived near us, so it was pretty easy for me just to turn inward.

As I've gotten older, I've broken through a lot of those early patterns, but I still find myself isolating and turning inward when I'm struggling or feeling at a low point. In my own faith journey, turning inward causes me to put my trust in myself and not in Jesus. When I fall into that mindset, I work hard and try everything I can to get things done and to be successful, because that's how I take care of myself.

Even now that I'm much older, I don't have a lot of people that I spend a ton of time with. I have friends that I love dearly, but it's easy for me to keep them at arm's length and not really let them inside. Similar to growing up, I know what to share and how much to share to keep people just outside of really knowing who I am.

WE OFTEN HIDE THE "REAL US"

For many of us, letting people know what's on the inside is scary. We wonder if people would still want to hang out with us or admit they're our friends if they really knew who we were and what we thought. It's easier to bury the true self and hide it behind an outer shell, because it provides safety.

But this is exactly what Satan hopes we'll do. I believe that our enemy wants to separate the outer and inner layers of our being because that disconnection gives him power—power to cause us immense doubt and pain as we struggle to maintain an outer shell that masks how we truly feel.

Here's the problem: When we don't let people know what's happening on the inside, they can't really get to know us. They are only encountering the "us" that we want them to see, which may not be consistent with who we really are. And maintaining an image can be so much work.

Living a stand-out faith in this fit-in world means drawing deeper connections between what you believe on the inside and how you act on the outside. It's not easy to be transparent and honest, but if you want to grow in your faith journey, it's vital that you become more transparent.

THINK ABOUT

What if you started to honestly tell people how you felt and what was happening on the inside? What kind of freedom might you experience if certain people in your life knew exactly what made you tick and could come alongside you because they knew when you were hurting and struggling? I imagine that this would be a great thing, and it would free you to let who you are on the inside be closer to who you present on the outside.

QUESTIONS

1. Which specific people in your life do you believe truly "know" you? Why?

2. Think of some stuff you just don't want anyone else to know—why are you reluctant to share these things with others?

3. How consistently does your interior faith in Jesus match up with how you portray yourself on the outside?

CHAPTER 3:
ARE YOUR FAITH AND LIFE CONSISTENT?

BAD CHOICES BY A "GOOD KID"

I remember the first time I ever made what I would describe as a really bad choice. My junior year of high school I went with two marginal friends (meaning we weren't very close) to a drive-in movie theater, and they had put all kinds of alcohol in the trunk of the car. Up to that point I hadn't really made many bad choices, and fortunately that night didn't end up too badly. But it was the first time that I knew I had to "hide" what I had done because if I didn't, people who thought of me as a "good Christian kid" were going to be disappointed.

Sadly, this wasn't the last time I felt like I had to hide things. I attended a small, private Christian college and always felt that I couldn't let people know fully what I was all about. I had a group of friends who went to another school and who had a lot of parties at their house. I went to all of them because these were my closest friends growing up and I felt like they formed my most important circle of friends. But I never took anyone from my college with me. It was almost like I had a hidden second life that I refused to share with them.

My college friends knew me as an outgoing and solid Christian who went to chapel every week and attended church every Sunday. What they didn't see was that I often went out Friday nights to my friends' house, clearly living a totally different life. I know God protected me and I never really made any huge, horrible decisions with major, painful consequences, but I also know that this dual life was one of the main reasons why I don't have many significant friendships left from my early years of college.

MAINTAINING AN IMAGE TAKES WORK

The funny thing is that I don't think I fully recognized how much this hurt me until I started reflecting on that last sentence. My faith and life didn't always match up, and that caused a whole pattern of hiding who I really was. I began to build an image that I wanted people to see—all while struggling to line everything up internally with what I actually believed.

I'm guessing you may be struggling with something here, too. You want to be transparent and honest, but your faith and your life have some sort of disconnect. Maybe it's not as serious of an issue as mine was, but any issue that gets between our faith and our life matching up can produce bad results.

My advice to you is to keep reading and reflecting about how you want to live. The ideas, strategies, and suggestions in this book can help you get to a place where things will line up better and where you will stop feeling the disconnect.

THINK ABOUT

I now live in the town where I went to college. It's been fun reconnecting with old friends. But there are still some friends that I wish I hadn't lost during my years of living that dual life. I wonder about the friends you have now from church and the ones that are from your school. Maybe they are completely separate groups of friends, and your church and school lives don't match up at all. Or maybe you go to school with a lot of your church friends. Either way, take a moment to think about how well your faith and your life line up—or don't line up.

QUESTIONS

1. On a scale of 1-10 (10 being highest), how much do you believe your faith and life match up right now? Why did you give yourself that score?

2. What areas of your life do you find hardest to talk to your "Christian friends" about, and why?

3. Are you doing things that you don't feel you can share with others? If so, what are some good, right, healthy ways to address those choices or actions?

4. What steps can you take to better align your faith and life?

CHAPTER 4:
DO YOU KNOW WHAT YOU'RE LIVING FOR?

AN IMPORTANT QUESTION TO ANSWER

What *are* you living for? Is that an easy or difficult question to answer? Can you immediately spout out a great reply that's exactly what you believe, or do you feel some tension to offer an answer that you think people would want to hear?

I've worked with teenagers for a long time, so I get it. You often feel backed into a corner, forced to share a tough answer to a tough question. You might feel like the little kid in Sunday school who just answers "Jesus" anytime his teachers ask a question—because there is a high percentage he'll be right. If you have a solid relationship with Jesus, then some part of you wants to answer that you are living for him. But if that's true, then you must wrestle with all the other stuff that seems to claim importance on your life, too. And if you are really honest, you likely endure days when Jesus doesn't seem like the answer, even though you want him to be.

As a junior in high school, my whole church world was turned upside down. Overnight, I went from having a really fun youth group experience to not having a youth pastor. It turned out that my youth pastor—who had taught me so much and loved me in practical ways, such as hanging out with me and asking me how I was doing all the time—was actually a flawed leader who ended up leaving his wife and moving in with his girlfriend.

The tough part is that I would've said he was living for Jesus up until all of that happened, but afterward I honestly couldn't tell you what I thought he was living for. That whole experience rocked my faith and made me distrust people for a long time. It also made me distrust myself and question what I thought I believed.

HONESTY IS TOUGH BUT NECESSARY

One thing I know about the Christian life: Sadly, it often isn't safe to be truly honest. You want to tell people that you don't get it or that you struggle to really believe God is who he says he is, but you just can't because people in the church don't always handle doubt well. So you hide it and keep offering Christian answers to the questions people throw at you.

Figuring out what you're living for can be tough because so many things compete for your time. You have school, sports, friends, family, work, church, and more—each taking priority at different moments. Often you have to make tough decisions and choose one thing over another. My advice is to spend a lot of time prioritizing the things in your life because if you don't, either everything will be equally important but unattainable, or you'll run yourself ragged because you're running around trying to do everything.

Faith has to be something that is important to you. I'm guessing it is because you are reading this book. But it can't be just another thing that you stuff into your backpack of accomplishments. It has to be something that's so real and a part of who you are that someone who barely knows you can look at you and in a few minutes have a pretty solid understanding that your faith matters to you. It must bleed from the inside to the outside.

THINK ABOUT

As you grow older, you are going to come across some "draw a line in the sand"-type moments when you must choose what you believe. You will benefit from figuring out what you believe before that happens. A practical example: You don't want to be trying to figure out "how far is too far" in a dating relationship when you are in a dark room with your significant other. Too many factors play into that decision—you want to make it in a safe, reasonable, thoughtful place.

QUESTIONS

1. Think of a specific time you believe you failed at the "what do you believe in?" question—what can you learn from that experience?

2. How have you been successful in sharing what you believe with others?

3. What are some specific things you do that help you wrestle with tough questions?

CHAPTER 5:
HAVE YOU MOVED BEYOND A "YOUTH GROUP" FAITH?

"A CHURCH OR A POOL HALL?"

I can still remember the moment when I got in the most trouble at church. I was a junior and we had just finished our 9:30 a.m. Sunday school hour. The general rule was that afterward, we all went together at 11 a.m. to "big church." That day we were kind of messing around in the youth room and lost track of time playing bumper pool. Next thing we know, the choir director (and dad of a youth group friend) came busting into the room and yelled at us: "Is this a church or a pool hall?"

He was so mad not seeing us in church that he had gotten up in the middle of the service to come and find us. He marched us back over to the church building—and needless to say, we never missed big church again. And it was good for me to be in church every week because it forced me to be "known" and to "know" the whole congregation.

Many people struggle to move beyond a "youth group faith." We grow accustomed to having an adult constantly contacting us and reaching out to us, encouraging us to attend events that are aimed at our age group. We like the messages that are focused on our life stage, and we find that a youth group surrounded by people our own age and stage of life is safe and fun and just makes sense.

LOOKING FOR A DEEPER FAITH

When I went away to college, I left my youth group behind, and it was really hard to find my place in any church. During my four years of college, I never got plugged into any specific church because I just didn't know how. I went to church every week, but never once did I do anything besides just sit in a pew or chair, listen to the sermon, sing songs, and then go home. I wasn't involved, engaged, or even really a part of anything.

And that pattern continued after college for a number of years. I finally got involved in a college/young adult group a couple of years after graduation, but it operated so much like a youth group that it just made sense that's where I would fit in.

Youth group faith is simple and easy. It's all about us, and it feels good. Stepping beyond that can be hard because we have to find our place in the church. I was never very good at that. Maybe you're better at it than I was. Or maybe your youth group and its leaders have done a good job of getting you connected to the rest of your congregation—and people who are there. Some churches do a phenomenal job at this. I'm always encouraged when I hear of churches that are engaging young people in the overall life of the church early, because I've seen that make a difference.

Moving beyond a youth group faith will take some work. You're going to have to commit to being a part of a broader context of church that isn't always about you. You may not always like the music, the sermon, or the dramas. You may be in some uncomfortable situations where you don't know how to interact or respond. But you and your faith will be better for it.

THINK ABOUT

If you didn't have youth group to attend, would you still go to church—or to *your* church? Think about that for a few minutes. You might be really connected to a small group, youth pastor, or other young people. If they weren't in the equation at all, what would your faith look like?

QUESTIONS

1. What does "youth group faith" mean to you? How might you define or illustrate that phrase?

2. What parts of your Christian journey will continue with you beyond high school—and what parts do you want to leave behind? Why?

3. How connected do you feel to the overall life of your church?

4. What might you do differently to get more connected?

CHAPTER 6:
CAN PEOPLE IN YOUR LIFE SPEAK TRUTH TO YOU?

THE REAL MEANING OF "FRIEND"

And...delete.

That's how easily you can get rid of a "friend" on social media. And it's only a little bit more difficult to add someone into your inner circle. Sadly, with the ease of adding and deleting people, many of us find that while our circle of "friends" seems to be increasing, the number of people who really know us and can speak truth into our lives—the real, true definition of a friend—seems to be shrinking.

As the world has become more interconnected and pluralistic, we seem to encounter so many more beliefs and ideas—and people are gravitating toward an even greater measure of tolerance and acceptance, to the point that right and wrong aren't clearly defined. It's almost as if we can't be truthful and honest with anyone anymore because our culture says we have to just let people believe and act however they want.

I didn't grow up in a world like this. I was probably more sheltered than anyone as I grew up on an island in Washington state. Everyone around me had a similar worldview and lifestyle, so it was easy to see when someone was deviating from the norm. I remember having friends who would question decisions I made or call me out when I was doing something wrong. That seems to be gone now as we're called to let people pursue whatever paths they want, even if they're drastically different from us—or different from what we know is right.

YOU NEED TRUE FRIENDSHIPS

Can people in your life speak truth to you and point out if you're headed in the wrong direction? I'm talking about the kind of people who have the freedom to call you out when you are messing up and don't have to sugarcoat it for you to listen. I once led a small group of guys who were all juniors, and the whole group had that kind of freedom to be honest and open with each other. I remember when all the guys told one guy in the group that he shouldn't be dating the girl he was. In fact, his buddies told him that *every single time* he came to the group. He didn't listen for about three months—but one day I think the group finally got to him, and he broke off the relationship. And everyone in the group told him he was doing the right thing. His reply: "I know."

I think it's rare today to have those kinds of friends. The sad reality is that we may be more "connected" to other people, but we aren't truly involved enough in the lives of people who can challenge, check, and encourage us to grow.

And guess what? This won't get any easier when you leave high school. I believe the online world and the way you can stay connected to people after high school often become a crutch that can keep you from investing in new relationships; you just maintain online ones with people who really aren't engaged in your life anymore. If you aren't careful, you can just slowly move into having superficial relationships with everyone. That's why it's so crucial to learn how to pursue and build meaningful friendships now.

THINK ABOUT

If you had an issue that you really wanted to talk over with someone right now, which people could you turn to? I can admit that I went through too long of a season in my life where my primary relationships were with people I wasn't doing life with anymore, so it was just kind of weird to go too deep with them because they didn't really know my life.

QUESTIONS

1. Think of two specific people in your life who can speak truth to you—how are you building and strengthening those friendships?

2. How do you usually respond when people call you out for something you are doing or are not doing? Why?

3. How have you spoken truth into a friend's life? How did that person respond?

CHAPTER 7:
ARE YOU TRYING TO FOLLOW BOTH GOD AND THE WORLD?

FIGURE OUT WHAT MATTERS MOST

I'm confident that you can relate to this one. You face so many competing things in your life every day that it's hard to not occasionally lose focus on God and turn your attention completely over to other things. And it's true that the messages you receive daily from our culture at school, on TV, on the Internet, and elsewhere reveal what the world values and what things our culture says "should be" your priority.

This is probably most apparent when you get to the end of your high school years and must make some decisions about your future. If you're planning to attend college, you've already been told about the importance of extracurricular activities, tougher classes, and a "well-rounded" résumé. So you feel the pressure to decide what is important and where you will put your limited time.

Maybe you find yourself stuck on a Wednesday night with too much to do and not enough space in your life to get it done. So you have to make a choice, and youth group is the easy thing to skip. Or maybe it doesn't even feel like your choice because your sports team holds practice on Sunday mornings and you just can't go to church anymore while still playing the sport you've been doing your whole life. And if life after high school means entering the workforce or the military, you face an entirely different set of pressures as you prepare for that next step.

CAN YOU BE BUSY BUT BALANCED?

Let me say this: There is nothing inherently wrong with extracurricular activities, sports, jobs, school, friends, or other ways you can spend your time. The only time those things become a problem is when they begin to take your focus away from God. And yes, I do think that it's OK for those things to be your focus occasionally—I'm talking about the big, overall focus of your life, sort of like the narrative that weaves through everything else you are doing. Is your faith in Jesus a constant in all you do, or is it simply one other thing on your list of important things that you do?

When I was in college, I was too busy. I worked several jobs, participated in sports, edited photos for my college paper, went on mission trips, and had a ton of friends. I attended a small, private Christian college, so you'd think I could have easily kept my eyes focused on Jesus, but it wasn't so easy for me. I found myself frequently distracted by everything I was doing, and Jesus often got moved toward the bottom of my priority list.

I'm hoping you aren't like I was, but you also may struggle with priorities and making Jesus the center of all that you do. If you don't and you have that piece figured out, then I encourage you to tell people how you do that, because your story and example could be teaching and helping others.

THINK ABOUT

Start putting together a list of all the things in your life that are important—write it here in this book, or on a blank piece of paper, or maybe just type it into your phone. As you examine the list, think about how the things you are doing make you feel. What are the key things that you just love to do, and how might you feel if you had to stop doing one of them? If you were categorizing your list from most important to least important, where would Jesus land—honestly?

QUESTIONS

1. How do you decide which activities, responsibilities, or commitments are important?

2. How much balance do you believe is in your life right now?

3. Where do you find Jesus on your list of things that are important to you? Are you satisfied or dissatisfied with that—and why?

CHAPTER 8:
DO YOU WANT JESUS TO MESS UP YOUR LIFE?

FOLLOWING JESUS WHEREVER HE LEADS

I have a friend named Phil whose life has been totally transformed by Jesus. Phil has worked with YWAM (Youth With a Mission) for about 20 years as a missionary here in the United States. He runs a ministry called "Steps of Justice" that is all about giving teenagers and young adults a vision for how they can make a difference in the world by caring about the things Jesus cares about. I met Phil on a mission trip to Seattle about 13 years ago. He was leading our team, and we became good friends and have maintained our friendship even though we've never lived in the same state.

Here's the deal: *Jesus has messed up Phil's life.*

What I mean is that Phil is totally sold out for following Jesus wherever Jesus leads. This last summer Phil led three teams of adults to

Cambodia to expose people to the hurts and troubles of a country that he loves. Last year he traveled around the United States towing a trailer with his entire family, just teaching about justice and leading worship/justice events.

Every time I talk to Phil, he's telling me something new that God is teaching him. He always seems to have a great listening ear, and God clearly is using him.

FOLLOWING JESUS CAN BE SCARY

Can I be honest with you? Sometimes Phil ticks me off. I find myself getting frustrated because he's so sold out that it makes my faith look so simple and basic. I think my biggest struggle, though, is that I'm terrified to let Jesus mess up my life like he's messed up Phil's life.

I like order and plans. That's probably a simple way to say I'm fairly controlling. I like things done my way, with my ideas and thoughts going into every action. I don't do well sitting and waiting for Jesus to show up and tell me what to do.

I'm scared to have Jesus step in and mess my life up *too much*. I like what I'm doing now. I've got a great church job, house, and friends, and I'm comfortable living in the Northwest. I feel like this is where Jesus wants me to be and that I'm doing what I'm supposed to be doing. If Jesus changes things too much, I'm not sure if I'm totally prepared to deal with it.

Think about your own journey now. You are approaching that season (or maybe you're already in it) when you will have to make some difficult decisions about your future. You are going to be applying for college or entering the workforce or joining the military. There are so many places you could go to school or jobs you could do or paths you could follow. The possibilities are really endless.

So how do you know what you are supposed to do? How do you respond? My wife recently reminded me that I need to trust Jesus more in the little things, so that's what I've been doing. How about you? Are you OK with Jesus messing up your life?

THINK ABOUT

Jesus can really mess things up in a good way. I know from following Phil's journey the last 13 years that God has been up to something with his life and there has been so much fruit. Jesus has even used my own story and my control issues to produce some tangible results in the lives of the teenagers I have ministered to. How comfortable are you right now with having Jesus change your plans and "messing up your life"? What plans or assumptions or dreams are you willing to let him change or transform?

QUESTIONS

1. How comfortable are you with allowing God to change your plans?

2. What are some things you believe you are following Jesus into faithfully?

3. What things get in the way of truly listening and following what God would have you do? What are some good, healthy ways to deal with these things?

PART 2
NEEDS

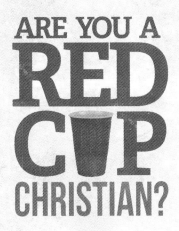

ARE YOU A
RED
C U P
CHRISTIAN?

Your faith needs to grow. You can't have the same type of faith journey as a junior or senior in high school that you did in elementary school or middle school. As your faith grows, you move beyond doing things just because you are supposed to be doing them. As your faith grows, your inward change becomes more obvious on the outside—people can see it. No longer are you like a red cup looking like everyone else—now you look like a real, living, breathing follower of Jesus who stands out in this fit-in world.

Our faith journey takes work—something we too easily forget. Oftentimes I find myself thinking back to my own high school years and reflecting on how my faith journey was lived out. Honestly, I can't remember a single talk that my youth pastor gave. But that didn't matter because I knew a few things about him.

First, I knew that he loved me and really wanted me to be around. When I missed youth group or found myself unable to go on a trip or retreat, he always called me to see how I was doing. Second, I knew he wanted me to grow. Even though I don't remember the talks now, I know that he spent a lot of time putting together messages and lessons that were aimed at reaching me where I was. I needed that. Third, I knew that all the volunteer leaders who were a part of our group really modeled what it meant to follow Jesus. More than anything else, that caused me to grow spiritually. They showed me how to be real, how to have the Bible relate to where I was, how to be real and honest, and how to let other people know me. They gave me opportunities to use my gifts and encouraged real relationships, not just silly games and simplistic thoughts.

In order to have a stand-out faith, we must recognize what we need. Faith is a journey, and we walk it every day. Sometimes we are walking alone, working on a few things, but other times we need people in our lives as we journey together. This section of the book is filled with topics and thoughts that will help you as you seek to grow your faith.

CHAPTER 9:
BEING REAL AND HONEST

WORDS OF WISDOM AND ENCOURAGEMENT

I recently wrote a letter to my son who turned 13. As part of his birthday celebration, we asked significant people in his life to write letters telling him who they see him to be. In my letter I talked about his leadership skills and the way God seems to have gifted him to lead people. But I also talked about my own faults and failures as a dad—the times I've struggled to best know how to love and care for him. I got choked up as I wrote the letter and was transparent about the kind of relationship I want us to have.

Do you find it easy to be real and honest? It doesn't always come naturally to many of us. We live in a world that teaches us to hide our true thoughts and feelings. It's almost like we are told to create a mask that we need to hide behind.

But as followers of Jesus, we have to be real and honest. In fact, I believe you *deeply desire* to stop hiding and to be more transparent with people. You know that it could make things so much easier if people just knew who you were and you could stop playing games. But that change also comes with fear—you wonder if people would accept you if they really knew who you are.

SAFE PEOPLE WILL HELP YOU GROW

To become more real, authentic, and honest, you need a few safe people in your life. Ideally, they should be people you interact with regularly, not online friends. I know that many of us have online friends that we share deep things with, and that can be good, but we need real, live, face-to-face friends. I often encourage students to get involved in some kind of small group where they will have a safe opportunity to be transparent with a leader or leaders and a group of other students. If your church doesn't have an official small group ministry, see if your youth pastor or a youth leader can help you find ways to connect with other people.

I had the honor of leading a group of guys from their ninth-grade year all the way through graduation. They are all 28 now and still find time to get together and talk about what they are going through in life. We created a space where it was safe for them to build real, honest relationships, and those friendships have continued—so awesome!

Being transparent is often tough because it means being vulnerable while hoping that the people you are sharing with will still accept you. One of the reasons so many websites out there offer opportunities to share intimate thoughts is because we are hard-wired to seek a place to honestly share. But we often don't feel safe doing it in real-life, face-to-face friendships, so an online, anonymous site becomes a "safer" place for us.

My advice is to take baby steps and to seek people in your life who will welcome your honesty—and will practice it, too. This doesn't mean sharing your deepest, darkest struggle in the first conversation. It's all about taking steps—practicing small doses of honesty and authenticity, and growing from there.

I recently had a heart-to-heart conversation with a few friends. I told them I really wanted to deepen our connection and talk about things that really matter. The responses I got were amazing, as both guys shared that they wanted to do the same thing—they were tired with the superficiality of it all. Sometimes all that's needed is *you* taking the first step in building more real, authentic, and honest friendships.

THINK ABOUT

The first step in being real and honest with other people is being able to do it with yourself. Consider starting with a journal where you write out what you are feeling and thinking. This can get you in the practice of being honest and real before having those kinds of conversations with other people.

QUESTIONS

1. Do you have anyone that you are open and honest with in your life right now? If so, how did that friendship develop?

2. How might you cultivate that type of relationship with some other people?

3. What's your biggest fear about building more real, authentic, and honest friendships?

4. What opportunities for connecting in small groups exist in your youth group or at your church?

CHAPTER 10:
KNOWING THE BIBLE AND LIVING IT

A SOLID FOUNDATION FOR LIFE

Jesus loves me, this I know, for the Bible tells me so. Now I know it and it's great, I'll learn some more at another date.

I kind of feel like those words reflect the general thought of many people in our culture. We learn a little bit about the Bible when we are young and then forget (or neglect) to keep learning as we get older. I'm more and more convinced that if we want to live a stand-out faith in this world, we must know the truths of the Bible and how Scripture connects to our real life. I'm not saying we have to stand on a street corner with our Bibles—I'm just encouraging you to be able to use biblical truths, which apply to the day-to-day stuff you face.

The Bible is a collection of writings that provide a solid foundation for us to stand upon. I wonder, if we are honest, how many of us might say we don't really know as much of it as we wish we did.

A SOURCE FOR ANSWERS AND WISDOM

As I've worked with students over the years, I've become more and more convinced that those who truly knew their Bible had a better foundation for knowing who they were than those students who didn't spend much time reading, studying, and knowing Scripture. Students in that first group were more open and honest, they knew where to turn for answers, and they were more confident. These were the students who could tell you what they believed and why. They weren't perfect, but most were living a stand-out faith.

Sadly, the exact opposite was generally true of students who didn't know their Bible or how to live it out. They didn't know what they believed, they struggled to find purpose and direction, and they were often overly concerned with fitting in.

"Living" the Bible means seeking to understand God and his role through Jesus of redeeming the world—and then living in a way that shows people that you believe God's work is true in your own life.

THINK ABOUT

When was the last time you sat down to read your Bible just because you wanted to grow? I'm not talking about reading because you felt you were supposed to, but just when it was something you wanted to do. My moment of honesty: Even as I wrote that question, I was convicted that my own Bible reading has not been up to par lately.

QUESTIONS

1. What's something specific you've learned recently from the Bible that you are trying to live out in your life?

2. Do certain barriers in your life keep you from reading your Bible on a consistent basis? How can you get rid of them?

3. What is a key book, chapter, or verse in the Bible that you consistently turn to when you need help in your life? Why do you return to that same spot regularly?

CHAPTER 11:
BEING KNOWN BY OTHERS FOR WHO YOU ARE

YOUR PERSONALITY CAN SHINE BRIGHTLY

When I was a junior in high school, I finally started to feel like I was coming into my own. Up until that point, I don't think I really knew what made me tick—and I'm convinced that if I didn't have it figured out, no one else really understood me either.

But that year something happened. I started to really take ownership of who I was, and my personality started to shine through more clearly. I started to figure out what I liked to do, and I did more of that. I was in a couple of bands at school, and my performances started to draw attention from the rest of the school. I became known as the "band guy," which at the time at my school was a good thing. People started to praise me for my performances and my talent. I also got some notoriety on a few sports teams and just kind of found my place.

Life sure became a lot easier. It wasn't work because I wasn't trying to be someone that I wasn't. I didn't have to put up a front or be a fake—I could just be me. That allowed me to be more comfortable in my own skin.

TRYING TO BE SOMEONE ELSE

That's totally different from the person I decided to become in college. When I made that transition, I decided I would become one of the outgoing, popular people. It was an actual decision I made, and it ended up being so hard on me. The biggest problem? I was successful at that goal.

I really became popular, and everyone knew who I was. I was even the freshman homecoming prince. I was popular but dying inside. As I've already mentioned, I'm actually an introvert so I tried to become something I wasn't, and that made things really difficult. People didn't know me for who I actually was—they knew me only for the front that I was putting up.

I don't know who you actually are. I'm hoping that others know you and they *truly* know you. It helps out so much when people have a picture of the real you and not just the person you are trying to be.

THINK ABOUT

We all can find ourselves acting differently in a variety of settings. You might have one personality at church and be someone completely different on a sports team or at school. The ultimate goal is that you would be able to be yourself in all situations.

QUESTIONS

1. Do you believe people really know who you are? Why or why not?

2. How comfortable are you at letting people know how you are really feeling?

3. Think about the various "yous" that people know—how can you become more consistent, so people truly know the real you?

CHAPTER 12:
USING YOUR GIFTS AND TALENTS

THEY'RE THERE; HAVE YOU FOUND THEM?

Pop quiz: What are your gifts and talents? You have three seconds to list them all!

OK, I'll admit that when I was in high school, I didn't have a really solid understanding of my gifts and talents—I would've failed that pop quiz just now. I knew I was gifted musically, but that seemed to only have real value when I was playing in a concert. It didn't feel like my talent had any particularly useful, practical application.

We all want to feel like we have something to contribute and that we make a difference. I can still remember the first time I really saw this played out, many years ago. I was on a mission trip to Mexico with my new church. When we got to the worksite, two junior girls were handed clipboards, and from that point forward, they were in charge of the two houses we were going to build. Somehow, someone had realized that these particular girls had the gift of leadership and the talent to pull off leading a large project. They were put into the perfect place for them to grow and lead.

YOUR GIFTS CAN BUILD YOUR FAITH

Discovering, developing, and using your gifts and talents is really important to living a stand-out faith. For a very particular reason, God has gifted you in specific ways. One way that you can draw closer to God is to use those gifts. It's like a scene from a classic movie, *Chariots of Fire*, where one of the characters says that when he runs he feels God's pleasure. God is pleased when you use the gifts and talents that he's given you.

Kevin was a student in my youth group many years ago. He was particularly gifted in music, too—but his gift was slightly more practical: He could play the bass and the guitar. When Kevin first started coming to youth group, he just naturally gravitated toward the musicians and the worship band. Before too long Kevin was sitting in with the band and using his gifts and talents to be a part. Kevin is still following Jesus today, and I think that's partly because he figured out how to use his gifts to glorify God.

You may not know exactly what your gifts are yet. That's OK. I encourage you to ask some

people who know you well what they think
those gifts or talents might be. After they tell
you, ask them how they think you could use
those gifts for God. They might have some
really great things to tell you and tips that can
draw you closer to God.

THINK ABOUT

From time to time, I wish I had a whole bunch
of different gifts. I imagine what I could do for
God if he would give me an extra dose of the
gift of leadership. And how much more useful
would I be as a pastor if God gave me the
talent of being able to memorize languages
easily? Well, it doesn't really work like that.
God gives us exactly what we need and seems
to know already how we might use it.

QUESTIONS

1. What are some gifts and talents that you
   know (or at least believe) God has given
   you?

2. How can you use those gifts and talents to
   serve God?

3. What have you already done with the gifts
   and talents God has given you? How are
   you developing and using them?

CHAPTER 13:
LEADING A LIFE FULL OF AUTHENTICITY

REVEALING THE "REAL YOU"

It can be hard to live a stand-out faith if we aren't really leading lives filled with authenticity. But I realize it's tough to be real in all situations. Most of us probably have "multiple personalities." That may sound like a very negative thing, but the reality is that we find ourselves behaving *differently* in a variety of settings.

I think back to my high school years, and I know that I was different around the guys on the football team than I was in my band classes. You, too, may find yourself acting one way around certain friends and differently around others. Some of those differences are OK, but you need to be careful that even in those differences, you remain authentic to who you are.

Think about it this way. If you are at youth group and someone starts to gossip about a person from your school, do you respond in a particular way because of the setting? Would you respond *differently* if you were sitting with friends at school, or working at your part-time job, or practicing with your teammates?

The goal is to be authentic to who Jesus created you to be—in all situations. Another way to think about this is that God wants you to be *consistent* in living what you know to be real, true, and right at all times. When you live a life of consistency, people know what they are getting from you at all times. They don't have to worry that you will respond completely differently in every situation, because they have already seen your authentic heart and know how you will react.

THINK ABOUT

Picture a specific situation that has happened recently. Would you have responded differently to the thing that happened or was said if you had been in a different location when it occurred? Are you the same person in the school lunchroom that you are in the youth group room? Are you the same person on a team trip that you are on a mission trip?

QUESTIONS

1. On a scale of 1-10 (10 being great), how authentic do you think you are most of the time? Why did you give yourself that score?

2. Identify a situation when being inauthentic hurt you with your friends. What can you learn from that experience?

3. What changes can you make in order to be more authentic in all areas of your life?

CHAPTER 14:
FAILING WELL AND HAVING OTHERS SUPPORT YOU

HOW DO YOU HANDLE FAILURE?

Failure will happen. Failure is OK. Failure is part of everyone's journey. Those may not feel like very encouraging thoughts, right? But keep reading...

You need to learn how to fail and what to do when it happens. One of the main reasons we put on an outward shell is because we don't want to let anyone see what we are really wrestling with. So when we fail, we often try to mask or hide it so that no one will know. That can work for a while, but it just puts us in that red-cup lifestyle where we seem like we have everything together on the outside, but internally we are struggling or falling apart.

Despite what some people say, not all failure is bad. In fact, really great failures can be springboards for amazing growth. I remember the first time I got up to speak to a group of teenagers about the Bible. I had put a lot of work into my talk and felt like I had written something that was going to change their lives—literally. Sadly, my talk was a total failure. First, it ended up being so short that I almost had to give it twice in order to fill the 20 minutes. Second, I had about eight main points, so I'm pretty sure that no student really understood what I was talking about. Third, I spoke way too fast, so if they had been able to follow along, it would've been really easy to get lost again because of my pace.

But I was fortunate that some very gracious and loving leaders in the room sat down with me afterward and gave me some constructive feedback and advice. I left that night's event feeling a little bit down, but because people had encouraged me, it wasn't a complete waste. I learned from it, and the next time I spoke, it was much better.

YOU CAN LEARN FROM FAILURES

We all need to grow, and sometimes failure is a great place to start. I'm not talking about huge, life-altering failures (although we *can* grow from those moments). I'm talking about putting yourself in situations where struggling helps you to grow in your faith.

Another example might be taking the opportunity to share your faith with someone who isn't a follower of Jesus. Maybe you have done that and felt like it just didn't go as well as you would have hoped. When you analyze what happened and consider what you might do differently the next time, that's the kind of failure or setback that you can really learn from and grow through.

If we aren't in places where failure can happen, it likely means we have sanitized our existence to the point that we are living a "safe" life and don't really risk anything. And faith has to be about risk and growth. Your faith won't grow if it never gets out beyond Sunday school lessons and youth group sermons. You need to take steps and challenge yourself so your faith can grow. But that comes with the risk of failure.

THINK ABOUT

What is something you would be willing to try in your faith journey if you knew that failure was a possibility but that the results wouldn't hurt you in any way? Would you be willing to take big risks for amazing potential payout? What would following Jesus into possible failure look like in your soul?

QUESTIONS

1. What's a specific "failure" you've experienced in your faith journey? What did you learn from that experience—or what *might* you learn from it?

2. How might you need to grow in order to be OK more with failure and growth?

3. What type of support network do you have for those moments when you decide to take big risks?

CHAPTER 15:
STEPPING OUTSIDE YOUR COMFORT ZONE REGULARLY

BUILDING YOUR TRUST IN GOD

One of the reasons I regularly take students on mission trips is because I know they're opportunities for teenagers to move beyond their comfort zone—while still remaining in a relatively safe environment. It's been shown over and over again that getting outside our comfort zone puts us in a place where we can really learn how to trust God.

When I was a junior in high school, I lived the first semester of that school year in Mexico. I wanted to be an exchange student, and I also wanted to really learn Spanish. Talk about being outside my comfort zone! I had grown up on a small island in Washington, and my comfort zone was pretty narrow. Getting on a plane by myself as a 16-year-old and flying to Mexico was a huge step. I figured out kind of quickly how to minimize my comfort level: by speaking English with one of the family members. They quickly caught on, though, and told me they wouldn't speak English to me anymore. So there I was in Mexico with a limited ability to speak Spanish, totally out of my comfort zone for four months. But you know what? I really learned Spanish. I also totally learned to trust God for comfort because I was so lonely.

FEELING UNCOMFORTABLE CAN BE A GOOD THING

You don't have to take that big of a step. Maybe for you, simply telling someone you are a Christian is a big step. Each person has a different level of comfort zone. The reality is that we all need to figure out where our comfort zone is—and then we need to simply be pushed a little bit to get outside of that.

We used to go to Mexico on a weeklong mission trip to minister in a village. I was generally really attuned to the group and knew how far each student was comfortable being pushed. So one student might be totally outside their comfort zone just riding in the van across the border, while another student might be the head of our vacation Bible school program. Each person filled a specific role, but it was a challenge for everyone nonetheless.

Being challenged will cause you to grow because it forces you to trust God. When you enter situations where you are uncomfortable or don't know how to respond, you can look to God to give answers. If you avoid these kinds of situations and choose to permanently dwell in your comfort zone, your faith will likely look just like everyone else's, and you'll end up like the red cup: The outside looks just like everyone around you.

THINK ABOUT

I'm guessing that at some point you've been pushed outside your comfort zone in your faith. You've been forced to rely on God, and he has come through. How did your faith grow?

QUESTIONS

1. How comfortable are you getting pushed outside your comfort zone for your faith?

2. Identify a time you moved outside your comfort zone in your faith. How difficult was it for you?

3. Where in your faith journey are you most uncomfortable being pushed and challenged? Why?

PART 3
SOLUTIONS

ARE YOU A
RED
CUP
CHRISTIAN?

As we move into the final section of this book, you may find yourself overwhelmed after thinking about the problems and your needs. Fortunately, I have good news: The solutions are not as hard as you might think. Yes, they will take some work and likely will require you to get outside your comfort zone. But they aren't impossible to pursue.

In each of the next eight chapters, I offer some specific tips, ideas, and strategies that can help you build and grow your faith. I advise you just to try out some of the things here. You might find that some ideas don't stick or really connect with you where you are. That's OK. Try something else. Maybe you'll land on something not even listed in this book but you'll get there from thinking through all of this.

I realize it may feel slightly arrogant to answer all the problems from earlier in the book with some seemingly simple solutions. My biggest fear is that you'll conclude that I have this all figured out. I believe that these chapters will help you, but remember that I'm still on my own faith journey, too—I'm also a work in progress.

Think of the next few chapters as "launching pads" that will simply give you places to start figuring it all out. Try some things, think about others, and see if you have any additional things that you want to try. And again remember: I'm on my own journey to figure these things out, too, so you're not alone in this adventure!

CHAPTER 16:
FIND A CHURCH THAT ACCEPTS YOU AS YOU ARE

It can be really tough to find a good, solid church where you feel comfortable. You may already be a part of one that you believe is a good fit for you—or you may feel the itch to change, to find a new church home. While you're still in high school, I don't advise you to switch churches—especially if this is a church you've been a part of for a long time. But after high school, you may find yourself needing to get rooted in a new church because of heading away to college or moving to a new town.

It's really important that you find a church that allows you to "come as you are" and to be yourself. Find a church that likes you for you, a place where you don't feel like you have to become someone or something else in order to fit in. If you like wearing sandals or tennis shoes to church, you probably don't want to start attending a congregation where everyone wears suits or fancy dresses. And if you care about deep, expository Bible teaching, a church aimed at seekers is probably not going to meet your need.

If you find the right church, here are some truths about what your experience can be like.

YOU WON'T HAVE TO HIDE IN A SHELL

Hiding in a shell isn't what you want to do at church—especially if you're serious about having a stand-out faith. If you find yourself constantly sitting in the back row, not engaging with people, and not getting involved in anything besides a worship service, there's a good chance you are hiding. There are appropriate times when hiding is OK—if you are simply needing some space and a break from everything—but there's a difference between space and isolation. In my opinion, being known is the No. 1 thing you need to do in order to continue to have your faith grow. And it is easiest to be known when you aren't hiding in a shell.

YOU WILL BE KNOWN

Does anyone at your church know your name or a little bit of your story? If you grew up at that church, then people probably do, but if you're attending a new church after high school, you will find out very quickly if you feel comfortable being known and letting people discover who you are. I attended five different churches during my college years but wasn't really known at any of them. This hurt me because I could have really benefited from the support, accountability, and programs offered by some of those churches. I really missed out because I was never known.

PEOPLE WILL PURSUE YOU

When the people of a church know you, there's a much higher likelihood they will pursue you and want to get to know you even more. When I finally committed to a church and let it be known that it was going to be my home church, the college pastor began to build a friendship with me. No longer was I just someone who was going to be floating in and out. I had made a decision to get involved, and the college pastor knew it when he talked to me. I soon was involved in weekly events and even went on a winter retreat. If you knew me then, you would be amazed that I had made that decision to get involved. But soon I had a whole bunch of people from the church who knew me and began pursuing me to keep me part of the congregation and get me more involved.

YOU WON'T HAVE TO BE LIKE EVERYONE ELSE

When people begin to know you, they will see who you really are. You won't have to look like everyone else and can truly be yourself. This is a huge step because it lets you avoid the rut of simply "fitting in." In fact, you'll find that the people you get to know in a healthy church probably won't *let* you simply fit in anymore. As you build deeper relationships, the real you will come out, and people will see how to best love and care for you to help you grow closer to Jesus.

WHO YOU ARE ON THE INSIDE CAN COME TO THE OUTSIDE

Authenticity is key in having a stand-out faith. You will be forced into becoming more authentic as you find a solid church and get involved. I'm not surprised anymore when I see that the students who are doing the best at living a genuine faith after high school are those who are the most connected to a church. People who get involved stay involved and have a deeper faith. You will have the opportunity to watch the real you on the inside come to the outside as you get involved and grow in a church body.

QUESTIONS

1. Why do you go to the church you attend now? What is most appealing to you, and why?

2. How well do you believe you are "known" by people at your current church?

3. Do you feel like the "real you" is allowed to come out in your current church? Why or why not?

4. How will you go about finding a new church if/when that time comes?

CHAPTER 17:
FIND PEOPLE WHO WILL HELP YOU STAND OUT

I have a friend named Evan. To call him a free spirit would be to be a slight understatement. But he's also one of the most honest and straightforward people I've ever met. When we were in high school, Evan was the guy who would call me out anytime he felt like I needed to be checked. That continued when we were in college, too. For some reason he just had this understanding of exactly when I needed to have someone speak truth into my life—and he was always there to do it.

I remember the time I just couldn't seem to figure out what to do about a particular girl I was interested in. Evan knew me well enough and had the freedom to ask a couple of really difficult questions that forced me to make a good but tough decision. Evan never let me get away with just skating by and looking like everyone else. I think he had some sort of radar so that every time I was starting to try to "fit in," he knew it—and would just nail me with his tough reminders.

I don't know if you have anyone like Evan in your life who can call you out, but if you don't, you definitely need it. We *all* need at least one of those friends. Here are some ideas on how you can build these kinds of friendships in your life.

BE MENTORED

One way of getting these kinds of people into your life is to find a mentor, and your church is a great place to start looking for one. Find someone who's eager to get involved in your life and help you as you're growing in your faith. It might be someone significantly older than you who has "been there, done that," or it could be someone just a few years older who is going through the things you will soon encounter. The goal of a mentor is to simply have someone you can talk with and ask for advice and ideas about what you need in your life and your faith. This needs to be a safe, trusted person you can talk to about almost everything. And you need to give this person the freedom to ask you really hard questions. A mentor sometimes will ask you things you really don't want to answer—but a good mentor knows that tough questions can lead to solid spiritual growth. If you can't find a mentor on your own, ask a youth pastor or just another Christian adult in your life if they know of anyone who can help you. Even as I wrote that last sentence, I thought about my own challenge to myself to find a mentor. It's been a few years, and I feel like I need to find someone who can help me grow. So I'm doing this one alongside you.

HAVE SAFE PEOPLE WHO CAN CALL YOU OUT BECAUSE THEY KNOW YOU

You need some safe people in your life who can call you out when you aren't doing right—people like my friend Evan. These are people who know you, know your story, know your life, and know what's important to you. Because they know you, they recognize when you are doing things that are risky, unhealthy, or unwise, and they love you enough to call you out when you need it. Who might fall into this category? It could be youth pastors, volunteers, coaches, teachers, trusted friends, and anyone else who knows you well enough that you've given them a role in your life and the freedom to question what you are doing.

GET INVOLVED IN A SMALL GROUP

This is a huge step to growth. I've been involved in groups most of my adult life. We didn't have them as an option in high school, but since then it's always been an important thing for me. During one season of my life, I was driving almost 100 miles in Southern California traffic to meet with a group of guys. That was a major commitment, but it was so good and so helpful. We prayed together, shared our hearts, and questioned each other when we needed it. Those guys had made a commitment to me—and I made that same commitment to them—and it really helped me in my 20s as I was making big, life-altering decisions about my future.

KEEP LONG-TERM RELATIONSHIPS

A key to lifelong spiritual growth is to maintain relationships with people you've grown up with—or at least people who've known you for many years. Unless you've been surrounded exclusively by people making risky, unhealthy, unwise decisions, you don't want to walk away from all your old friends and start from scratch. Use the relationships you have built to continue to build you. If you've moved away from your hometown, this means you need to meet up with your old friends when you go back for holidays. Tell them what's going on, and get their honest feedback about what you are doing. Using social media to stay connected to older friends and youth leaders can be good (as long as you are still building new relationships) because it'll help you maintain a connection between your high school life and your life beyond high school.

QUESTIONS

1. What adults are involved in your life, and how do they help your walk with Jesus?

2. What people in your life can call you out when they see you making unwise choices or heading in the wrong direction? If no one fills that role, what steps can you take to build those kinds of friendships?

3. What positive or negative things have you experienced from being involved in a small group?

4. What is something you can do to have more people in your life who will help your faith grow?

CHAPTER 18:
BE ENGAGED IN ACTION THAT SHOWS WHAT YOU BELIEVE

I'm always thinking about how my faith can be expressed in action. Over the years, I've participated in a whole bunch of mission trips and service days. I remember one day that was so powerful and really taught me about Jesus and how he wants me to live. We were crossing the border into Tijuana to set up showers for a small community. About 15 of us were on the team, and it took a lot of work to get everything set up. Most of the families in this village didn't have running water, so taking a shower was a pretty big deal.

After we got everything set up in these tents, the team leader asked me to find a couple of students who could wash the feet of each boy as he came into the tent. I found two of my high school guys, and for the next two hours they sat on benches near the opening to the tent and simply washed the boys' feet before they went into the shower. Talk about a powerful image—and something that absolutely translated faith into action for those high school guys.

What faith-in-action moment can be equally powerful for you? Maybe it's simply making the decision to join a campus Bible study or sitting next to someone at lunch who is seen as an outcast. Putting faith into action looks different for each of us, but it is a huge step to growing your faith and making it stand out amid this fit-in world. Here are some specific thoughts.

FOCUS ON SERVICE AND THE THINGS JESUS CARES ABOUT

Jesus cared an awful lot about serving other people. So did the early Christians. In order for your faith to grow, you must get outside your comfort zone (something we've already discussed) and live like Jesus lived, love like Jesus loved, and serve like Jesus served. Service can include a variety of things, but generally it falls in the area of helping other people. How can you help others now, or after you've graduated? What could you do that helps you look beyond yourself and focus more on other people?

BE WILLING TO TAKE RISKS

One great way for your faith to grow is to take risks—put yourself in situations that nourish your faith and trust in God. I remember taking some students to San Francisco one year. We came around a corner and saw more than 200 men lined up, waiting to get into a mission to have lunch. My white, suburban, upper-middle-class teenagers were terrified that day. But three days later, they were standing in that same line interacting with the men and telling them that Jesus loved them, even in their difficult situation. My guys took some risks, and God fully used them there.

GO ON A MISSION TRIP

Being young gives you a great advantage: You generally have free time to do things that older adults can't always do. You likely have fewer commitments holding you back from getting out and serving on a mission trip. I want to encourage you to get out there and try it. It doesn't have to be a two-week trip to Uganda; it could simply be a one-day trip to downtown Seattle, New Orleans, Chicago, or New York. Either way, you are serving, and it's an opportunity to serve people and share the message of Jesus. I'm convinced that one of the best ways to grow in your faith is to passionately, frequently get involved in mission trips.

SERVE YOUR CHURCH

I've already mentioned that I did a poor job of getting connected to any church in the first few years after high school. Because of that, I missed out on the opportunity to grow by serving. But as a youth pastor I've worked with hundreds of volunteers who have shown me how getting involved and serving in a local church can produce a huge impact. My wife, Danielle, was a volunteer at her church, leading a small group of girls when I met her. Those girls were so blessed to have a solid woman of God who loved them and walked alongside them for all the years they were in high school. Serving your church is a great way to move beyond being a pew sitter and turn your focus from you to others.

SERVE WITH A LOCAL MINISTRY HELPING THE NEEDY

In college I got involved volunteering at a local shelter for men that got them off the streets of Seattle each evening. My college partnered with this ministry a lot, and it was something I loved to do. I found that serving in my city was a great way of seeing the world through the eyes of Jesus. This kind of service can change your perspective and give you a bigger heart for the city where you live.

SERVE SOME FOOD

Food is basic and a great way to connect with people. On that trip to San Francisco years ago, we did what we called a "love feast," where we served food to the homeless and then also sat with them and asked them to tell us their stories. You see, everyone can feed someone, but engaging people in honest conversation while they eat is a whole different thing. I encourage you to start with the basics because food opens doors to ministry.

QUESTIONS

1. Think of a specific time when you felt especially close to God through serving— what did you learn from that experience?

2. How can service change the way you think about your faith?

3. Are you currently participating in any service or mission opportunities? If not, how can you find some?

CHAPTER 19:
STUDY THE BIBLE AND UNDERSTAND HOW IT RELATES TO YOUR LIFE

Understanding the Bible more fully will deepen your faith. A deeper faith will help you grow into more of the person Jesus wants you to fully become. The opposite is also true: A shallow understanding of Scripture leads to a shallow faith. Here are some ideas on how you can more deeply study the Bible and absorb its life-changing truths.

GET INVOLVED IN A BIBLE STUDY

I'm involved in a group study that meets every other week—a bunch of dads going through one chapter of Romans at a time. It's the right rhythm for us to get together, and Romans is so deep that we find we can only get through one chapter at a time. Studying the Bible with other people is important to growing your faith because they will often push you to look at the Bible from a different perspective. They also may ask questions that you might not think about on your own. There are many different ways to do a Bible study. You can do it in the morning at a restaurant, or in the evenings at someone's house. It can be formal and follow a specific program, or less structured and built around the needs you have at the time. You can have a leader (or not). You could go straight through a book of the Bible or follow a devotional or topical series. What matters most is that you are studying the Bible alongside other followers of Jesus.

REALLY LISTEN TO THE SERMON

This sounds so basic, but I know that for many high school students, actually listening to the sermon may not be something that you do very well. I'm encouraging you to listen to the sermon that your pastor preaches each week. Look for connections between that sermon and ones you've heard before. See what main points your pastor makes, and analyze how it all compares with the passage of Scripture when you read it. Check out the verses, and see if they make sense and draw you closer into the sermon. If you're unable to go and hear the sermon, your church probably records them and you can listen to them on your own—your church may even have its own podcast. And once you're trying to find a church after your high school years, it's helpful to listen to sermons from different churches before picking where you will attend.

READ YOUR BIBLE ON A REGULAR BASIS

Another moment of honesty: I struggle to read my Bible on a regular basis at a consistent time. I wish I were a first-thing-in-the-morning or just-before-going-to-bed guy who read his Bible and had that structure. I don't—and I know it hurts me. What I try to do is just keep a Bible near me—either in my car or just on my phone—and read when I make time. So when I'm sitting waiting for my kids in my car, I'll pull out my Bible and read a chapter or two. Reading your Bible and knowing Scripture will help your faith stay at the center of who you are and keep it flowing out of you.

LOOK THROUGH YOUR CHURCH LIBRARY OR A CHRISTIAN BOOKSTORE

I like to read biographies of Christians that I respect. I read a great one on author C.S. Lewis that really helped me understand his writing better. I'm a reader and love to browse bookstores and libraries looking for things to read. If your church has a library, you may be able to find some great books that will help you grow. But because church libraries are notorious for having older books, you might have to go to a library or check out a bookstore's Christian section for newer books.

ASK OTHER PEOPLE WHAT THEY BELIEVE

There was a time in my life when I *loved* getting into discussions and asking people what they believed. Dialogue was important to my Christian growth, and I found it through asking questions and talking to people. I found it helpful to get a different perspective from someone else because it would either affirm my own views or challenge them. This might take you way outside of your comfort zone, but it'll really help you grow.

MEET WITH A PASTOR TO DISCUSS WHAT THAT CHURCH BELIEVES

I wish I had done this more when I was looking for a church. Hearing the pastor share what a specific congregation is all about and what it believes would have helped me find a church and get more involved. Instead, I just picked churches that had elements I liked and started going without really knowing anything else. And sometimes, when I slowly figured out what the church was all about, I realized its focus was completely different from what I believed. Talk about awkward! So take a step of faith, and as you are looking for a church, call up a pastor and ask to speak with him or her. I can almost guarantee the pastor will want to speak with you!

QUESTIONS

1. If you've been in a Bible study, what were some of the benefits?

2. How often do you read your Bible? What might help you to read it more consistently?

3. How can you find out what your current church believes? How might meeting with the pastor help? (Then go do it!)

CHAPTER 20:
BE IN COMMUNITY WITH OTHERS WHO KNOW AND LOVE YOU

Community is something we all crave. We want to be known by others and to see that our presence makes a difference. We desire authentic, real relationships with people who know exactly who we are—and love us nonetheless.

I've been involved in several groups of people like that over the years. During my second year of college, my family was going through a particularly difficult time. One day I ended up sitting in a friend's room just crying—and over the course of about a half-hour a great community of people whom I loved and who loved me all gathered to pray for me and my family.

The best way to get this type of community is to actively get involved in groups and places where it can happen. Church is a great place to look. Churches often have programs and plans in place to help young adults find community. It's something many churches do really well. Here are some thoughts that can help you as you seek true community.

GET INVOLVED IN A SMALL GROUP/LIFE GROUP

Whatever name or label a church uses, this is a group of people who simply have decided to experience life together, hang out on a regular basis, and talk honestly about how they are doing. The whole point is to be known and to know each other. That's why regular meetings with open and honest conversation are really important. You may still spend some time studying the Bible as a group, but the main focus is being in community with other people. Finding this type of group can be hard, but knowing where to look can make it a lot easier. First, check your church—you'll likely find some great options for getting connected. After your high school years, you might look at such ministries as College Life, Navs (The Navigators), Cru (Campus Crusade for Christ), and others. Generally, there is some sort of meet-and-greet day where different college ministries gather and you can get to know some people. Local churches might set up booths on the campus, too, and that can be a good place to start asking questions. If you want community, getting involved in a small group/life group is a must.

JOIN SOMETHING AIMED AT YOUR AGE/STAGE OF LIFE

A church in the town where I went to college had a ministry called The Inn that met weekly for a time of worship, Bible study, and fellowship. Each summer the ministry sent out missionaries all over the world on a program called deputation. The Inn was an amazing ministry with hundreds of students—and it was all aimed at my age group, so they really got me and understood the stage of life that I was going through. Look for ministries that are aimed at students in late high school and college because they're most likely to be in tune with your needs and will have programs and activities aimed at helping you grow.

BE TRANSPARENT AND REAL WITH PEOPLE

The best way to grow with others is to be real with them. I'm learning this more and more as I get older. Just yesterday I had an amazing heart-to-heart conversation with our middle school pastor; I was honest about how I was doing, and he prayed for me in his office. We're colleagues at my church, but we're also friends and fellow followers of Jesus. It's amazing how much depth occurs when you are real and transparent with other people.

WORK TO BE KNOWN

Being known is a little bit different from just being transparent. Being known means people fully understand what makes you tick. They are aware of how you might respond in situations and know how to best interact with you. Being known means that someone has gotten beyond the shell of your exterior and sees the real heart of who you are. This is tough to do, but you do it every time you tell someone about yourself and share a little bit deeper about what makes you tick.

QUESTIONS

1. What priorities or values do you think would be most important for a small group or life group to display, and why?

2. How have you benefited from being honest and transparent with other people?

3. When do you find it easy to be transparent with people? When is it difficult?

CHAPTER 21:
PURSUE MORE THAN JUST A "YOUTH GROUP" FAITH

I think youth group faith can be a great thing—up to a certain point. When you are in youth group, it's fine if you have that kind of faith. People cater to your needs and interests. A specific leader focuses on getting you involved and encourages you to attend events and activities. When you aren't there, people miss you and someone might actually call you and tell you that.

But from a long-term, big-picture perspective, that isn't the kind of faith that will sustain you when you leave youth group. The "real world of church" generally doesn't have a leader who is tied to your age group. You probably won't get reminder calls or follow-up notes. The messages taught won't be directly aimed at your age and stage of life. But all of this is OK because that's how it's supposed to work.

Take ownership of your faith. Take responsibility for growing in your faith, instead of relying on other people to feed you spiritually. Ask the Holy Spirit to reveal to you the message you are supposed to be hearing. When you get beyond a simple youth group faith, you will find an incredible richness in your Christian walk that increases in depth. Here are some suggestions and ideas that can help.

GO TO A WORSHIP SERVICE

Finding a worship service or church service that you connect with can be tough. If you're still in high school, then go to your church's service (or one of its services, if you have options). If you find that you don't really connect there, check out another church at a different time. The goal is to find a place where you feel comfortable and where God speaks to you. After high school, it is really important that you quickly find a church. If you go away to college or move to another town after graduation, the statistics aren't in your favor if you wait very long to find a church. My best advice is to try two or three different churches and see which one feels right. Then attend regularly and keep going.

GET TO KNOW OTHER ADULTS IN THE CONGREGATION

Once you've left high school, you really are an adult. That's why it's important to get to know other adults within the congregation. How? One of the best ways is to simply find out what they are doing and get involved. So if your church has a men's ministry or a women's ministry, this can be a way to get involved. Yes, you will likely be the youngest person there, but with that notoriety probably comes some excitement from the other adults to get to know you. Why is this important? Because you can learn a ton from people who are older than you. They have been through much of what you are going to experience, so why wouldn't you want to learn from their successes and mistakes? Just take a look at anything that your church offers (or the church you are considering being a part of). Find out what things they are doing and see if they appeal to you—maybe a multi-generational mission trip, car club, service group, or some other ministry.

JOIN WHATEVER GROUP IS NEXT FOR YOU

If you just finished high school, your church likely has a college or young adult group that you can join. You may feel like everyone is so much older than you. If that's the case, find some other people your age and talk them into going with you. Don't try to hold on to youth group. If you go away to school, when you come back for the holidays, try to connect with a group that is aimed at your life stage. You're entering a season of life filled with transition, but this doesn't mean you have to lose all your friendships and connections. Stay in touch with your youth pastor and other volunteer leaders, even though those relationships will change. They are no longer "your leaders," and you will slowly start moving into a peer relationship with them. If you need help, ask them how you can get connected to the group(s) that will benefit you. If you've gone away to school or moved to another town, find the right age group for yourself and get involved.

BE A SELF-STARTER

This requires some big steps on your part. Maybe you've been in a youth group where you received constant reminders and updates about what was going on, and youth leaders may have called and texted you every time there was an event or activity. This won't happen as much as you get older, so you will have to be a self-starter and get yourself to where you need to be. This is a big step in the maturing process of your faith. It becomes about you taking charge of it.

DON'T RELY ON YOUR YOUTH PASTOR TO SUGARCOAT THINGS

This was probably the hardest thing for students who were in my youth groups to deal with after they graduated. The role that I had played in their lives for many years was suddenly gone, and they had to figure things out on their own. At times, I had been the person who would explain how things worked in the church, and I even sugarcoated things occasionally—but that ended when they graduated. Once you're an adult, it's unlikely that you will have that one leader who is in charge of you anymore or anyone who will take on that role. After high school, you may enter into a ministry that has a dedicated leader, which could make it feel very much like youth group, but for your faith to grow you're going to have to move beyond that and take the initiative on your own.

QUESTIONS

1. How much of a self-starter are you when it comes to your faith? Think of some specific examples.

2. How do you think you'll do if you don't have a youth pastor (or someone filling that kind of role) to help guide your steps in your faith journey?

3. What role can your friendships play in helping you through that stage of your faith journey?

4. What can you do now in order to prepare for the time after high school when your faith becomes much more about your initiative?

CHAPTER 22:
EMBRACE A FAITH THAT DOESN'T JUST BELONG TO YOUR FAMILY

I'm not sure how it happened; but my faith in high school was pretty independent from my parents. I got myself up to go to church and youth group and just relied on them for rides to get there. Church wasn't really a family thing in my house after my elementary years. We went occasionally as a whole family at Christmas and Easter. But the foundation that my parents had started in me at a young age definitely helped me make church a priority—and that helped me in my faith.

I don't know how it is for you. Maybe you only go to church when your parents are pushing you to get there—if it were up to just you, you might not make it there. At some point in late high school and definitely after high school, you must rely upon yourself to go to church and get involved. Your parents won't play a significant role in getting you up out of bed and off to church anymore. Here are a few tips that might help you make your faith a little bit more of your own.

BE KNOWN AT YOUR CHURCH INDEPENDENT OF YOUR FAMILY

At some point, being known as "Larry's son" was a good thing for me because it identified to a lot of older people who I was, but eventually I had to make the transition to simply being known as "Lars." You'll need to figure out how to be independent of your parents at church and be known as an individual. I'm not saying that your family isn't important or that you should never be identified with them. I'm just saying that it is a both/and type of situation where you need and want to be identified as a person on your own—your personality and who you are must be revealed apart from your family identity. How do you do this? You could get involved in things that the rest of your family isn't involved in. Join the choir or sing in the worship band if you have that talent. Serve in the child care center or go on a mission trip with others. Just find places that feel right for you to get involved and choose to jump in.

GO TO CHURCH EVEN WHEN YOUR PARENTS AREN'T GOING

Here's a great question to get asked at church: "Where are your parents?" If you go to church one morning and they aren't with you, then you may gain some points with whoever asked you about it. At that moment, people will realize that your faith is beginning to become your own, that it's more than just your parents' faith. Growing up, I went to church a lot without my parents. And I was very involved at my church, too. Ultimately, you will get to a stage in your life where you don't have the opportunity to go to church with your parents, so practice motivating yourself to go when no one else is waking you up, telling you to get dressed, and getting you out the door. Motivate yourself.

USE YOUR GIFTS AND TALENTS

One great way of embracing a faith that's truly yours is to discover and develop your gifts and talents, and use them to serve in the church. If you are gifted at teaching, then teach. If you can clean, then clean. If you love being with young kids, then get in the nursery. The more you figure out what you do well and what you love doing, the more you will find that the church becomes *your* church and not just the church that you attend because your parents go there.

QUESTIONS

1. What role has your family played in your level of involvement at your current church?

2. Once you have to make the choice for yourself, what type of church will you be looking for, and why?

3. What are some differences you've experienced between going to church with your family and going without them?

CHAPTER 23:
ENGAGE YOUR DOUBTS AND QUESTIONS

One key step in developing and demonstrating a stand-out faith is to be OK with doubts and questions. I remember a season in my own faith journey, during my sophomore year of college, when I experienced some major doubts about God. Ironically, it was the same year that I held a ministry position at school! My family was going through some difficult things, and I remember just wondering why God would let these tough things happen. In fact, I remember very distinctly at one point wondering if there was really even a God at all.

Fortunately, I regularly met with a couple of older students who created a safe space for me to doubt and ask all the questions that I had. And they didn't always try to answer my questions. Sometimes it was enough for me just to have someone listening when I shared what I was feeling—just getting it off my chest was enough.

Unfortunately, in some communities of faith, doubt is frowned upon or even feared, so we hide it within us and don't share it with others. That, in part, causes the red-cup syndrome where we feel like we need to look a certain way on the outside, even though on the inside we are struggling with our faith. In this final chapter, we'll look at a few thoughts that can help you as you wrestle with and engage doubt and questions, and how that experience can help your faith to continue growing.

BE OK WITH DOUBT

Doubt is not a bad word or an inherently bad thing. At some point, we all find ourselves questioning things about our faith. Maybe you've endured a really difficult family situation or a medical problem. It might simply be the reality that we live in a broken world and horrible things happen, and you wonder where God is in all of that. I'm not sure what triggers your doubt, but I do know that having safe places to express doubt is a healthy component of growth. In fact, faith usually requires some amount of doubt in order for us to really trust in God. If everything were spelled out and simplified for us, we wouldn't really need faith, right? And remember that God is OK with doubt. We find plenty of passages in the Bible where people doubted God, where the disciples didn't fully understand what Jesus was saying, or where people didn't fully grasp who Jesus was. Just read the Gospels and you'll see that Jesus was really OK when people had doubts or didn't fully understand.

FIND A SAFE PLACE TO ASK QUESTIONS

This is one of the main reasons I push the idea of mentorship and small groups. These relationships offer a safe place where you can ask honest, tough questions. The goal is to experience the freedom that comes from addressing questions or concerns that you have. I'll be honest: Doing what I did in college—only being engaged in a church worship service but no other part of the church—is the exact opposite of what I encourage you to do. It's one of the reasons as a high school pastor and now as a family life pastor that I go on extended trips with students where I can build relationships that can pave the way for them to ask me tough questions. And now that I'm older, I'm not afraid to say, "I don't know, but I'll walk with you through this time of doubt." That leads me to my final thought...

LOOK FOR PEOPLE WHO ARE WILLING TO TALK AND ENGAGE WITH YOUR DOUBTS AND QUESTIONS

If you're still in high school, I hope that you are connected to at least one trusted adult (ideally, more than one) who will listen as you ask questions, express your thoughts, and share your feelings. And if you've left high school, you can benefit from similar friendships in a small group or with other trusted leaders or friends, as we've already discussed. You may find that it's tough to find people you can talk to. This could be particularly true if you're joining a new church. You may be looking around, feeling isolated and wishing you could share with people honestly. My advice is to get involved at the church and see if God provides those people through your involvement. Maybe someone in a ministry where you serve will seem like the right person to approach about being a mentor. Or maybe you'll meet a group of people who feel like they could become your small group/life group.

QUESTIONS

1. How do you handle your biggest doubts and questions? Are you satisfied or dissatisfied with how you handle them? Why?

2. What are the key characteristics you'd look for in someone you'd feel safe sharing with honestly and openly?

3. How can you go about cultivating relationships with people who can help you sort through your big questions about faith?

CONCLUSION

I really wish I could return to that scene in Austin, Texas, with all the college students standing around with their red cups. Only this time, I wish God would give me some sort of X-ray vision so I could see into their hearts. I'd really want to have the power to view them as they really were, separated from any images they were attempting to portray.

The unfortunate truth is that we all fall into the trap of feeling like we can only show people a small part of who we are. And that part is often so easily covered up by the world. Living a stand-out faith in this fit-in world takes work. You will have to get involved in a church, pursue a faith that isn't just your parents' faith, deal with your doubts and questions, and move beyond the youth ministry faith that has catered to you for years.

But it can be done. You can have a vibrant faith. You can transition from high school and take your faith with you. You can break free of the red cup and live a Christian life that is visible on the outside—and literally changes your life. I believe you can do it, and

I'm excited to see you making steps to grow. God is good all the time and will stay with you through all your transitions.

As you take steps aimed at growing your faith, you might encounter some of the problems that I described in the first section of the book. Go back and reread those chapters and reconsider the questions. Each question is aimed at giving you a reminder about the action steps you can take to overcome the problem.

None of this is easy, but with Christ all of it is doable. You can achieve a stand-out faith in this fit-in world—a faith that is real, exciting, and vibrant. You can build a faith that people will see when they look at you—a faith that will continually transform your life.

ARE YOU A
RED
CUP
CHRISTIAN?